Be a Master at Communication

Be a Master at Communication

Debra Valdez

Bald and Bonkers Network Academy

Copyright © 2024 by Debra Valdez

All rights reserved. No part of this book may be reproduced, distributed, or transmitted in any form or by any means, including photocopying, recording, or other electronic or mechanical methods, without the prior written permission of the publisher, except in the case of brief quotations embodied in critical reviews and certain other noncommercial uses permitted by copyright law.

Published by Bald and Bonkers Network Academy, an imprint of Bald and Bonkers Network LLC
ISBN/SKU: 979-8-3302-7032-3
EISBN: 979-8-3302-7033-0

Artificial Intelligence was used in the editorial process of this book.

First Printing, 2024

CONTENTS

1. Introduction — 1

2. Considering Verbal Communication — 2

3. Considering Nonverbal Communication — 5

4. Using Effective Communication — 7

5. Be Intentional in Your Speech — 9

6. Be Brief and Specific in Your Words — 12

CONTENTS

7 Final Thoughts 15

Introduction

Mastering the art of communication is a crucial step towards becoming an exceptional leader. Effective communication skills are fundamental for those who aspire to lead and make an impact. Without these skills, one's ability to lead effectively is significantly hindered.

This concise report outlines the top five strategies for honing your communication skills. While these are not the exhaustive means of mastering communication, they represent the most effective methods for enhancing your communicative abilities and, consequently, your leadership qualities.

2

Considering Verbal Communication

Effective verbal communication is crucial for leaders, whether delivering a speech or guiding a team in the workplace. The words chosen and how they are conveyed often form the basis of others' judgments. Poorly chosen words can lead to misunderstandings or negative perceptions. It's essential to ensure that all verbal interactions are clear and adapted to the audience's needs.

In terms of vocabulary, it's beneficial to use a broad range of words that enhance communication without overcomplicating the message. Even for well-educated audiences, an overly intricate speech can be tedious and disengaging.

It's crucial to tailor your vocabulary to your audience. The manner in which you communicate is equally as significant as the content of your message. Emphasizing key points and using the appropriate tone and pace for the subject matter at hand is essential.

Your delivery can captivate an audience. By analyzing speeches from notable leaders, you'll observe a pattern: they often whisper to underscore subtleties and raise their voice to highlight important points.

Emotion and enunciation play crucial roles in verbal communication. While displaying emotion can enhance the impact of a speech, it is distinct from becoming overly emotional. It's important to harness emotion to strengthen your message while simultaneously managing it to avoid discomforting the audience.

Being an effective leader involves speaking with

clarity and precision. Enunciation is key to ensuring that the audience comprehends your message. Strive to articulate each word distinctly, avoiding any tendency to mumble or let your words blend together in a way that might sound forced or unnatural.

Considering Nonverbal Communication

It is often said that nonverbal communication can be more impactful than the actual words spoken. Many individuals may not fully consider their nonverbal cues. It's important to be mindful of your posture and hand movements when engaging with others.

For instance, rather than keeping your arms rigidly at your sides throughout a conversation, utilize hand gestures to emphasize points and indicate objects of interest. However, be cautious not to overdo it. Recording yourself while speaking can be an effective strategy to observe and refine your nonverbal communication skills.

Eye contact is a powerful tool in communication. When engaging with an individual, maintaining eye contact is crucial. In contrast, when addressing a group, it's important to scan the room to include everyone in the conversation.

Your posture and arm positioning are equally important. Avoid crossing your arms, as this can appear defensive. Instead, adopt an open stance with your arms and body to welcome interaction with your audience.

Regarding the preference for standing or sitting during a speech, it often varies. Most speakers stand to better engage with their audience, but some may choose to sit, depending on the context of the discussion and the audience involved.

Using Effective Communication

Effective communication requires understanding its core principles. Here are key considerations for communicating effectively:

● Audience Awareness: Tailor your language and approach to fit your audience. The way you communicate with children, for example, will differ significantly from how you address adults. Align your language with the audience's understanding.

● Message Purpose: Define the objective of your message. Whether it's to persuade, uplift, or inform, the content should be crafted to achieve this goal. Consistency in your message reinforces clarity and understanding.

● Communication Method: Choose the appropriate medium for your message. Social media, emails, or professional meetings each serve different purposes. Select the method that best suits the nature of your communication.

● Consistency: Maintain a consistent tone and style in your communication. This not only helps in making the message clear but also ensures that the audience feels engaged and not confused.

● Desired Outcome: Be clear about what you aim to achieve with your message. Establish metrics to gauge the effectiveness of your communication to ensure it is being received as intended.

● Diverse Perspectives: When crafting your message, consider various viewpoints, especially in a workplace setting. This inclusivity can enhance the message's relevance and reception.

Be Intentional in Your Speech

Being intentional signifies that your communication is purposeful, with a clear design and objective. It involves having a strategic plan for conveying your message in a manner that motivates and influences your audience.

Every word you utter, whether to a single individual or a larger audience, should carry a genuine message and intention. A speech lacking in substance will be transparent to listeners, who will then disengage and ignore the content.

Intentionality extends beyond mere words; it encompasses the actions that support and validate your statements. For instance, if you advocate for budgeting and financial savings, it is crucial to demonstrate that you practice what you preach by being prudent with your own finances.

An audience's perception of a speaker's financial credibility can significantly impact their receptiveness to the speaker's advice on finances. If they are aware that the speaker is in debt or lacks investments, they may be less inclined to be influenced or motivated by their financial guidance.

This underscores the importance of crafting your message with care and deliberation, especially on topics where your personal practices are visible to others. As a leader aiming to improve communication and intentionality, it is crucial to demonstrate to your team that you embody the principles you advocate.

For instance, when communicating the necessity for enhanced customer service within a business, it is crucial that both the audience and employees witness you exemplifying superior customer interactions.

Without a commitment to improving customer relations starting at the company's highest level, it becomes increasingly challenging for employees to be motivated to follow suit if they do not see a model to emulate.

Hence, it is imperative for leaders to be deliberate in their thoughts and actions while crafting speeches and other influential communications.

Be Brief and Specific in Your Words

Mastering effective communication crucially involves being concise yet precise. This is particularly vital when delivering speeches to an audience. Lengthy speeches that meander through unrelated topics can quickly diminish audience engagement.

Therefore, whether addressing a public gathering or speaking to your team in a meeting or presentation, brevity is key. It's essential to cover all necessary details and points, but they should be conveyed clearly and without unnecessary repetition.

Once an audience begins to doze off or becomes distracted, it's extremely challenging to regain their focus. Therefore, it's crucial not to lose their attention from the start. This principle is applicable to both written and spoken forms of communication.

Ensure that your entire message is included and presented in the most logical order. That's why rehearsing and practicing speeches and presentations beforehand is advisable. You aim to deliver your message coherently, avoiding the need to circle back to points you may have missed initially.

When responding to a question, it's important to formulate your response before you start speaking. This approach ensures that you can provide a complete and coherent answer, reducing the risk of omitting any significant points.

Projecting authority and clarity not only commands attention but also garners trust from your audience, a crucial element of effective leadership.

However, the challenge of being concise yet precise is a common hurdle. Mastery of this skill requires diligent practice, particularly for those who find it difficult to distill their thoughts into unambiguous directives.

The key lies in the ability to be succinct without sacrificing specificity, achievable through careful review and rehearsal of your intended message. Often, elements believed to be essential may merely prolong the discourse unnecessarily.

Therefore, it is advantageous to initially test your speech with a smaller, familiar group, such as friends or family, before presenting to a larger audience.

7

Final Thoughts

Mastering the art of communication may appear challenging, yet it becomes more attainable when you adhere to the five key tips and steps outlined. Achieving proficiency in communication equips you with the ability to influence and impact others significantly. As you aspire to become a motivational speaker, it's crucial to hone your communication skills, not only with those close to you but also with broader audiences. Moreover, as a leader in the workplace, it's imperative to master communication to garner respect from your employees and to convey your messages with clear intent.